D1260990

Live to Tell

Live to Tell

The Trial, Conviction, and
Exoneration of Anthony Wright

Anthony Wright with
Rob G. Kelly

To order additional copies of this book, contact:
Xlibris
844-714-8691
www.Xlibris.com
Orders@Xlibris.com
815316

CONTENTS

PREFACE

Imagine being framed and set up by the police. One day, you are snatched from society and then nearly executed by way of lethal injection by the Commonwealth of Pennsylvania for a heinous crime you absolutely did not commit.

Imagine losing all you have ever worked for; leaving your young child, a big family, and all your friends behind; and being sentenced to life in prison without the possibility of parole for a crime you absolutely knew nothing about. This is not only my reality, but this is my story.

In the early 1990s, many found it hard to believe that the police officers who were sworn to protect and serve the community would go through drastic measures like planting blood and DNA evidence, fabricating and falsifying reports, coercing witnesses, and threatening defendants to make and sign false confessions, and committing perjury to make their cases stick. When all this happened to me, I was quickly convinced that not only does this happen, but it happens even more than society realizes, and the corrupt police officers committing these crimes and foul acts are not being prosecuted.

After serving nearly a quarter of a century in Pennsylvania's toughest prisons, which seemed like forever—with attorneys Barry Scheck, Peter

Neufeld, and Nina Morrison (all lawyers of the Innocence Project) believing in my innocence—DNA testing exonerating me of the vicious crime of the rape and murder of an elderly woman, and a second jury acquitting me of all charges, I walked out of prison on August 23, 2016, a free and innocent man. After so many hopeless and lonely nights, so many rejections of my innocence by the police, district attorneys, courts, judges on all appeal levels, and my first jury who got it wrong, I finally came out victorious.

When a Philadelphia prison guard called my name for release and I took that long walk down that dim corridor, escorted by prison guards, I could not help but have flashbacks of my horrible nightmare of being escorted by state officials to the death chamber and strapped down to a gurney to be executed for a crime I did not commit. But I snapped back to reality when I heard the jingling keys from the guard opening the exit door. When my feet hit the concrete, the whole world seemed to stop and then begin to move in a slow, dreamy state. I took in my first breath of fresh air as I felt that special warmth from a bright sun and saw all my loved ones welcoming me back home after being gone for so long. I hugged and embraced my son, Anthony Wright Jr., and my family, lawyers, friends, and supporters. I kissed my granddaughters, one-year old Romera Wright and eight-year-old Daria, on their chubby cheeks, and spoke with the press. After, my dad, David Parker, and son said, "We are taking you home now," it was undoubtedly the best day of my life.

CHAPTER 1

As a child, I had a special love for the game of football, and I played football all throughout my teenage years on the streets of North Philadelphia. In the 1980s, my mom, Marilyn Martin, sent me down south to the state of Georgia to spend time with my dad. There, I enrolled in the Organized Football League, which was a league that prepped young players for college and pro football. Soon, I gained buzz for being one of the league's lead scoring running backs. My coach was so impressed with my performance that he contacted his associates in the National Football League to tell them about his quickest and most elusive running back, who he believed belonged in the pros.

My hopes and dreams of playing in the NFL, however, were shattered after I returned to Philadelphia in 1991, where I was charged with a capital murder.

I later learned that the victim was Mrs. Louise Talley, a seventy-seven-year-old widow who lived alone in her home on Nice Street in North Philadelphia. She had a well-known presence but kept to herself and tended to her small garden. I further learned that on the evening of Friday, October 18, 1991, an intruder (who the police claimed was me) entered Mrs. Talley's home, obtained a knife from the kitchen, and took Mrs. Talley to an upstairs bedroom, where he vaginally raped and anally sodomized her, stabbed her repeatedly, and delivered a crushing blow to her face with the hard heel of a shoe. The intruder stole various items from Mrs. Talley's home, including two televisions.

The next day around three o'clock in the afternoon, when neighbors had not seen Mrs. Talley, they contacted the Philadelphia Police Department about their concerns. Officers from the Thirty-Ninth District were the first to arrive. After police officers entered Mrs. Talley's home, they discovered a gruesome and bloody scene. Philadelphia homicide detectives Dennis Dusak, Manuel Santiago, and Thomas Burke arrived shortly thereafter. Their inspection of the crime scene, police reports, and later testimony revealed that Mrs. Talley was discovered facedown on the floor of her upstairs bedroom, naked and bludgeoned. Strewn about the body were various items of bloody clothing, including her nylon stockings, girdle, and shoes. Underneath her body were her blood-soaked empty purse, blouse, bra, and housecoat. She suffered ten stab wounds to the front and back of her body. Defensive wounds on her arms were also evident, indicating a struggle had occurred.

The crime scene further revealed what the police believe was the murder weapon, a twelve-inch metal kitchen knife with an eight-inch blade, stained with blood and wrapped in the folds of a pink bathrobe next to Mrs. Talley's corpse.

Detectives Dusak, Santiago, and Burke further discovered what they believed to be masculine-looking items of clothing: a black Chicago Bulls shirt, jeans with a front black suede patch, and black Fila sneakers that were worn by the killer. These items would wind up being vital pieces of evidence that would help prove my innocence.

While at the scene, Detectives Dusak, Santiago, and Burke learned that individuals around the neighborhood had seen two men, Roland St. James and John "Buddy" Richardson, attempting to sell Mrs. Talley's stolen televisions. The detectives quickly learned that both men had criminal histories of drug use and were suspected of operating a crack house a few houses down from Mrs. Talley's home, where they allegedly provided rooms to local prostitutes to turn tricks.

An officer from the Thirty-Ninth District determined that Roland and Buddy had been in possession of Mrs. Talley's televisions and other stolen items. They were later located, arrested, and taken down to the Philadelphia Police Department's homicide unit. After being initially interviewed by Detectives Baker and Morton to gain detailed information, Roland and Buddy were interviewed a second time and concocted a story that falsely implicated me as Mrs. Talley's killer when they knew the actual identity of the real killer, who would later be revealed through DNA testing. Afterward, Detectives Baker and Morton let Roland and Buddy go, even though Roland had an arrest warrant out for him for an unrelated matter, and they were never charged with their possession of Mrs. Talley's stolen property.

Next came my arrest for capital murder.

CHAPTER 2

It was Sunday, October 20, 1991. I was in the living room, chilling with my son, Anthony Jr., watching football. After the one o'clock kickoff, there was a knock at the door. Detectives Santiago and Burke appeared, introduced themselves, and said there had been a murder in the area. They politely asked me to come down to the homicide unit to be interviewed and said they'd bring me right back. I knew that I hadn't killed anyone.

On the ride down to homicide, my mind began to wonder. Whom did I know who was recently killed? Growing up in North Philly, I had been affected by so many killings. I had lost friends, associates, and schoolmates to street violence. Was this some cold-case murder investigation? Then it dawned on me that the detectives had said there had been a murder in the area. That seemed to mean a recent murder, and I honestly did not have the slightest clue about any recent murder or why they would want to question me.

When we arrived at the police administration building, I was taken upstairs to the homicide unit. The mood instantly changed. Detective Santiago ordered me into a small, stuffy interrogation room and accused me of murdering a lady named Mrs. Talley. I told him I knew nothing about it, and I had an alibi witness. He became enraged and left. He soon returned with Detective Burke, and they lashed out at me, accusing me of raping, sodomizing, and killing Mrs. Talley. They claimed they had eyewitnesses and physical evidence against me, which I knew was impossible.

"You're a fucking lying bastard. We know you did it, and we will be sure to prove it!" Detective Santiago screamed.

"We already know the answer to the questions we ask, Tony!" Detective Burke chimed in. "We've been doing this too long to let a punk like you outsmart us. So, you better fess up!"

"I ain't do it. I ain't do it. I innocent!"

"You ain't leaving out of here until you admit it!" Santiago yelled, banging his fist on the table before me.

This heated exchange went on for what seemed like hours. Then, dripping with sweat, they up and disappeared.

Soon after, however, they returned to go through another heated exchange for about another two hours.

"I need a drink. I need a smoke," I let them know.

"You will get that only after you confess!" Then they disappeared again.

What I did not know was that they'd called in reinforcements: the infamous homicide detective Martin Devlin, who had a reputation of obtaining murder confessions by any means necessary.

When Detective Devlin opened the door, he walked in slowly, holding some papers in his hand and studying me with piercing dark eyes. He was a tall white man with a thick mustache. He appeared angry—as if he were me, being held against his will for hours and interrogated to confess to a crime he did not commit. Detective Devlin moved closer to me, placed the papers he was holding before me, and then put a handcuff on my wrist and handcuffed me to the chair. "We know you stabbed that old lady to death," he said. "After you sign this paper, you can go."

I said, "No ... no ... no."

"You will sign it, boy," he said, pressing his nose against mine. "You will sign it, or I will skull-fuck you, boy! Do you hear me?"

"I ... want to call ... my mom," I let out.

"She can't help you. No one can. The only thing that can help you is if you sign that paper."

Detectives Santiago and Burke appeared again and shut the door behind them. One of the detectives pressed on the back of my neck as Detective Devlin flashed a devilish grin. Then he let go. I exhaled and then took a deep breath of air. I was filled with exhaustion, shock, and terror by then. I had never been part of or seen anything like this. Not only was I still chained to the chair, I was outnumbered and tired, and I wanted out.

The trio then took turns pressing me, taunting me, threatening me. I held out as long as I could until I had had enough. It was at that time that I made the worst mistake of my life. I signed the paper that Detective Devlin had placed before me. I just wanted it all to go away so I could go home, like they said.

I never did go home. Instead, I was booked for capital murder. I later learned that the paper I had signed was a nine-page confession that was prepared by Detective Devlin, stating that I raped, stabbed, and killed Mrs. Talley, that there was no forced entry, that I wore a black Chicago Bulls shirt, blue jeans with a front black suede patch, and black Filas during the crime, and that these clothes were currently in my bedroom at my house. In retrospect, I couldn't believe what I had done. I was furious, mad at myself. How in the world did I let them manipulate me as they did?

A jailhouse lawyer later said, "This is a capital murder, man. A signed confession to a rape and murder of a seventy-seven-year-old lady is like signing your own death warrant."

I knew I messed up bad, and it would be almost impossible to fix. The only thing I had left was my trump card: that I was innocent.

CHAPTER 3

After my official arrest, I ended up at Holmesburg, also known as "the Bird," located in Philadelphia County on State Road. The Bird was a notorious old jail, built in the late 1800s, that become known for housing high-profile Black Mafia, Italian mob members, and other gangster figures. The jail cells and units were filled with rats, mice, roaches, and other annoying pests. In 1991, it was also the place where all the city's capital murder, rape, and other violent detainees were forced to eat, dwell, and live together. Many gangsters did not survive in the Bird's prison general population long enough to make it to trial before being murdered or charged with a jailhouse murder. Others were chased into protected custody.

In the early 90s, a collective task force had made the arrests of several members of the Junior Black Mafia (JBM), which according to the prosecutor's press conferences was a violent organized crime syndicate. Many of the JBM members were awaiting trial and confined at Holmesburg, along with other organized gangs from all parts of the city, so according prison staff, the violence at the Bird was steadily increasing.

For me, the worst thing about being in a kill or be killed environment like the Bird during this time was I was innocent. There were at least five to six stabbings per week. I saw it all unfold, knife for knife, blood dripping onto the concrete, and bodies going out in body bags.

There was another problem. I was charged with the rape and murder of an elderly woman—a Black woman at that. Rapists are among the most despised individuals in a prison setting. Not only did my mom raise me to respect women, but I had learned how much our Black women had gone through during slavery in this country and what my ancestors like Harriet Tubman, Sojourner Truth, and Rosa Parks endured in the struggle for freedom. So, I had a special respect for my elder Black women.

It pained my heart knowing what Mrs. Talley must have gone through when she was viciously raped and stabbed to death by an obvious lunatic, and it made me physically sick just thinking I was being accused of such a gruesome and cowardly murder that I could have never committed. My heart also went out to her family, although they expressed their hate toward me. I understood that they rightfully would feel that way, as they were misled by the Philadelphia Homicide Division detectives.

As I learned more about the murder through court filings and proceedings, my first thoughts were it seemed like the act of some desperate drug addict, and some two decades later, DNA testing would prove my intuition to be correct. Thing was, I wasn't a drug addict or a junkie and did not fit that profile. There I was, however, in the heart of the Bird.

To survive in a place like the Bird, I knew I needed a shank. So, I got two. I was ready to fight and preserve my own life. I had to. How else would I prove my innocence and get back to my family?

I further learned that rapist pretrial detainees would also receive an enormous amount of flack from the prison guards, who had access to detainees' street charges. Many of the prison guards and staff were from the same urban streets of Philadelphia and believed a defendant would not be awaiting trial for a rape or murder charge unless he was in fact a rapist or a murderer.

I learned more and more each day how important it was for me to clear my name. It was my goal. Being an accused rapist and a murderer of an elderly Black woman from North Philly had to be the worst thing in the world. In addition, a nice percentage of the prison guards were Black women from Philadelphia. Many of them had a great influence over the male prison guards as well as the male prisoners they knew from their neighborhoods.

Once the word got out to the prison population about my charges, I maintained my innocence, but the drama came. The first physical encounter was when I returned to my cell after showering. There were two big intruders awaiting me. I fought hard and long for my life and dignity—so much for "innocent until proven guilty." When it came to being accused of rape at the Bird, you would be guilty until proven innocent and tested. I was bloody and busted up bad, but so were they. I was no punk, and they let that become known.

A few months after that, I got shanked, but I fought back and used my weapon. I adjusted and adapted quickly. I learned that in the jungle there were a lot of hyenas, and the only way to keep the hyenas off you was to be the lion. So, a lion I became.

My mom came to visit me once when I had a swollen lip and a swollen eye. She said, "If something happens to you in here, your blood will be on those crooked cops' hands that framed my baby for this horrible murder." She knew there was no way I could have committed a crime like that. She never wavered on my innocence. She also informed me of the details of the night of my arrest when three detectives arrived at our house with search warrants, headed upstairs to my room, and seized my white work jumpsuit and framed pictures of the family.

My son's mom, Lisa Rambert, would bring Anthony Jr. up to visit me as well. The visits were short. There was never enough time to cover Lisa's issues, our son's issues, and my issues and to prepare for trial to get out. The prison system was set up that way by the prison architects and wardens—to keep you in.

I had a lot at stake. If I lost my trial and was executed, my son would be losing his father to a corrupt system and would be left to fend for himself without me. I knew without me there, there was a greater chance he would wind up in prison himself after being raised on the streets of Philadelphia. At night, I would ponder the big picture while in my cell after visits.

CHAPTER 4

"**W**ake up, boy! Them white folks is gonna shoot you up with battery acid for killing that old lady, you damn fool!" I was awakened by the taunting words of Old Man Henry, a prison guard at the Bird who worked the graveyard shift. He was dark skinned, sported a gray-haired flat top, and wore thick Coke-bottle glasses.

"You're wrong, old man. I'm innocent!" I replied.

I got little sleep most nights, and I surely couldn't sleep during the day. I had to stay awake and alert to my surroundings.

Morning came quickly. After the powdered eggs and grits at the chow hall breakfast, I headed to the law library.

Out of all my problems, one of the most significant was the obvious—I could not afford to pay a good trial attorney to save my life.

"It's extremely hard for a poor man to find justice in an American court." These are the words from a poem written by Rob G. Kelly. These words rang true.

I learned that most public defenders do not have the same resources as good attorneys with supported law firms and that some public defender attorneys would only do the basics to defend you. Pennsylvania pays the attorneys at the public defender's office some of the lowest wages in the country. Most of the attorneys at the Philadelphia Public Defender's office had big caseloads and could only dedicate a limited number of hours to each case. Of course, the detectives who framed me for this murder were well experienced with the system and knew without a great trial defense team, I would most likely be convicted and executed with the fabricated evidence they concocted against me.

After reading a few law cases, I headed back to the block.

The next day, I received a visit from my court-appointed attorney. I let him know that I was 100 percent innocent and that I needed him to help me beat these charges. We spoke about the aspects of the case and the criminal justice system.

A defendant in Pennsylvania charged with a capital murder offense had to pick a "death-qualified jury." That meant all the jurors had to state before the court that they had no absolute ideological bias against capital punishment and were willing to vote for death if the aggravating circumstances outweighed any mitigating factors. The problem I learned with death-qualified juries is that statistics show that they are more prone to convict than the average juror. Therefore, the typical jury of your peers that you would ordinarily have on the jury pool would be excluded if they simply did not think they could vote to kill you. One jailhouse lawyer recommended to request the ordinary twelve jurors to decide the innocent and guilty phase, and if they came back with a first-degree conviction, a death-qualified jury also seated aside would decide on the punishment after the first twelve jurors were excused.

Although many attorneys recognize and assert that death-qualified jurors deciding the innocence or guilt phase violates the Fourteenth Amendment to the United States Constitution, my court-appointed attorney, Bernie Siegel, did not raise the issue.

Instead of attacking constitutional violations, his focus was on the case facts and whether I would testify on my own behalf. Under the United States Constitution, every criminal defendant in America enjoys the right to testify in his or her own defense and has the right to confront his or her accusers. A criminal defendant also has the right to be informed of this by both his attorney and the court. Many attorneys, however, advise against some criminal defendants testifying on their own behalf because it provides the prosecutor with an opportunity to bring out facts he or she normally could not get out before the jury. One of those main facts is that it exposes any prior criminal convictions that were of crimen falsi (for example, fraud or theft by deception) or prior bad acts of the defendant.

I instantly felt the jury should hear my side. I was innocent and felt that I needed to look the jury in the eye and tell them that. If I missed that opportunity and was convicted, I knew that I would regret it. There are other jury biases that would come into play, I learned, that came with my taking the witness stand. One or all the jurors might not like how a defendant talks, walks, their lack of emotion, or their lack of shedding a tear for the deceased. With all this in mind, I made it clear to my attorney that I wanted to take the witness stand on my own behalf.

The other thing was because Mrs. Talley's killer had both vaginally and anally sodomized her and stabbed her repeatedly, after the jury took her elderly defenseless age into consideration, they would likely want the perpetrator to pay the ultimate price. Therefore, if the jury came back with a first-degree conviction in my case, Attorney Siegel would need to try humanizing me in their eyes (if that was at all possible). One way, would be to put my parents on the witness stand to explain how I was as a child, paint out all my good deeds, and essentially beg for the jury not to kill their child.

This really bothered me and had hit home. These detectives not only tried their best to destroy me and get me executed, but they also destroyed my family, and my family was as innocent as I was. I wonder if the cops took all of this and the fact that I could be murdered while awaiting trial at the Bird with an agitated population of both young and old accused murderers into account when they set me up.

There were other problems with being housed at the Bird. With so many fights and stabbings, they would lock the place down frequently. There were A, B, C, D, and E blocks separated by F, G, H, I, and J blocks. When you heard, "Going down on both sides," come over the prison intercoms, that meant lockdown—there would be no law library for legal research, no showers, no recreation, and no phone calls or visits for a while. When the lockdown was lifted a week later, we would be out for a few days and get locked down all over again. When I got a chance to make it to the law library, I would get legal information from jailhouse lawyers who worked there. Many of them were very intelligent men who had missed their callings and had helped free several of their fellow prisoners. Many pretrial detainees were skeptical about being represented by public defenders and did not trust them, especially for capital murder beef. I was absorbing all the new information quickly.

When I wasn't in the law library, I was lifting weights and boxing in the gym. This kept me busy and in shape. If you needed to talk to your attorney, woman, or child on the phone, you had to be ready to fight or use your knife. There was very limited phone time on the three direct phone lines and two collect phone lines that were to be shared by more than one hundred men. The phones were run by the prisoners and assigned geographically. If you were from North Philly, you used the North Philly phone, and if you were from South Philly, you used the South Philly phone, and so forth. Most confrontations were related to the phone use, or lack thereof. Many times, this would escalate into big geographical gang and knife wars that would result in, sure enough, bloodshed, lockdown, and even death.

What a way to live, I thought. Yet, this was what my life had come to. Next, I had to begin preparing for trial.

CHAPTER 5

I had a visit with Lisa and my son shortly before my first day of trial. Young Anthony asked, "Daddy, why you been in jail so long? When are you coming home?"

"I'll be home soon, Son," I replied. How do you tell your child who needs you in his life that you can't be there because you were framed by the Philadelphia Police Department for a very serious crime?

"He asks for you every day, and all day. I don't know what else to tell him or what else to do." Lisa began to sob. I studied the tears that fell from her eyes, and for the first time, I shed tears of my own.

"This ain't fair," Lisa continued. "Do everything in your power to get out of here, Anthony. I really mean that."

When my day of trial came, I was ready to be acquitted of all charges and reunite with my son, family, and friends in society. Being confined nearly two years at the Bird was also taking a toll on me. Prison guards woke me about 3:30 a.m. to go to court. I didn't have much of an appetite, so I just drank my coffee and some OJ in the chow hall and headed to the receiving room pen. There, the receiving room prison guard gave me a suit, tie, socks, and shoes that my family had left for me. About two hours later, I was handcuffed and shackled to other detainees on the transport bus headed to the Criminal Justice Center.

About 9:30 a.m. that morning, I was seated in court beside Attorney Siegel. My family was seated directly behind for support. In the next at aisle were the family and friends of Mrs. Talley. It seemed like their piercing eyes that were glaring at me were burning holes through me from behind. I could not wait to be acquitted of the false charges so they would finally know the truth.

Judge D. Websterkeogh was an all gray-haired man who wore round glasses. He was known as a no-nonsense judge and had told both sides he expected them to play by the rules that he set forth and to move forward with their cases before the jury was called in. During the death-qualified jury process, each juror said he or she could vote to kill me if the aggravating circumstances outweighed any mitigating factors, and then the trial was on its way.

The prosecutor opened first.

"Ladies and gentlemen of the jury, the evidence will show that on the evening of Friday, October 18, 1991, Mr. Anthony Wright entered Mrs. Talley's home on Nice Street in North Philadelphia. He obtained a knife from the kitchen, took Mrs. Talley to her upstairs master bedroom, where he vaginally raped and anally sodomized her. Afterward, the defendant viciously stabbed her ten times in the front and back of her body with a twelve-inch metal kitchen knife. Ladies and gentlemen, the evidence will show that Mrs. Talley fought back, and a struggle ensued. The evidence will further show that on October 19, 1991, Mr. Wright confessed to this heinous murder to the police and signed a nine-page confession, which I intend to admit into evidence, along with the murder weapon. In conclusion, after you review all the evidence, I will ask each of you to return a guilty verdict for first-degree murder and recommend the maximum punishment under the law in Pennsylvania, and that, ladies and gentlemen, is death!"

I heard someone gasp in the row where my family was seated. The judge shot the person an admonishing look, and then my attorney, Mr. Siegel, rose out of his chair and addressed the jury with his opening statement. He asked the jury to find me not guilty because I was not the person responsible for the crime. He told them that the state could not meet their burden—proving beyond a reasonable doubt that I was in fact the person responsible for the crime.

After this, Judge D. Websterkeogh instructed the Commonwealth to proceed. The prosecuting attorney first called the Thirty-Ninth District officers who were the first to arrive on the murder scene, followed by Homicide Detectives Santiago, Dusak, and Burke. They each described the crime scene in detail to the jury. Detectives Santiago, Burke, and Devlin also testified that I confessed to the crime and signed a nine-page confession describing the crime in detail, including details that only the killer would have known. None of the detectives told the jury that they had threatened to rip my eyes out and skull-fuck me while they put their hands on the back of my neck if I didn't sign the statement prepared by Detective Devlin.

The medical examiner testified that the manner of death was homicide, that a rape kit was collected that included swabs from Mrs. Talley's rectum and vagina. But the test was inconclusive. Years later, however, newly advanced scientific testing revealed there was sperm in Mrs. Talley's vagina and rectum that matched another man.

Next, Detective Burke testified that he located three fourteen- to sixteen-year-old witnesses from the neighborhood, and they implicated me as the person entering Mrs. Talley's home wearing a black Bulls shirt, jeans, and black Filas, and they signed police statements to Detectives Jastrzembski and Antonio Johnson, indicating the same. This testimony made my blood boil. I knew these detectives had forced and manipulated these kids to say this. I expressed this to my attorney, and he replied that this was hard to prove. Evidence years later would reveal that the detectives violated police regulations when they questioned the minors without the permission or the presence of their parents, and they threatened the young boys.

The next day, the trial resumed. The Commonwealth called Detective Baker to the witness stand, followed by Detective Morton. Detectives Baker and Morton testified that they interviewed and took the statements of Roland St. James and John "Buddy" Richardson, and they implicated me as being the perpetrator. I knew they were lying through their teeth, and I hoped it was as obvious to the jury as it was to me. Detectives Baker and Morton never told my attorney, the court, or the jury that they had evidence in their possession that both Roland and Buddy were in possession of Mrs. Talley's television and other stolen property that linked them to the crime and that they let them go home, even though Roland had a warrant out for his arrest. I learned about these crucial facts years later.

Next, Detective Jastrzembski was called and testified that he and

Detectives Anthony Tomaino and Thomas Augustine conducted a search of my mom's home after obtaining a search warrant, and they recovered a black Chicago Bulls shirt, blue jeans with black suede patches, and black Fila sneakers; that all these items appeared to have blood on them; and that testing of the blood substance was consistent with Mrs. Talley's blood but not my blood type. I whispered to my attorney, reminding him that they never gave my mom a receipt for any of these alleged items seized, and my mom had witnessed them take a white jumpsuit and photographs from my room, not these items that they were misrepresenting to the jury. Evidence revealed years later indicated that the detectives planted one minute drop or smear of Mrs. Talley's blood on the jeans and the Bulls shirt to fit their theory of the crime, which, of course, the detectives hid from my attorney, the court, and the jury.

Attorney Siegel was not only for the conspiracy the Philadelphia homicide detectives had concocted against me to make their theory of the crime stick. The truth of the matter was neither was I. Seeing it on paper and hearing and seeing the testimony of numerous decorated detectives back over each other and their scared, coerced witnesses corroborating their testimonies seemed very convincing, I had to admit. I knew that it would take a dream team of experienced lawyers to pick the case apart to get to the truth. But I was not giving up that easily. During the break, I told Mr. Siegel that I still wanted to testify.

"I see the fire in your eyes. But this will be a lot tougher than I anticipated," he responded. Attorney Siegel had cross-examined each of the witnesses, but it didn't seem to score many points with the jury.

The next day, I testified on my own behalf. All eyes were on me when I headed for the witness stand. I knew everything was on the line. I did nothing more than tell the truth—that I had absolutely nothing to do with the crime. I did not know Mrs. Talley, and I was very sorry to hear what happened to her. I had been with a friend, Joseph Harris, at a nightclub called the N.A. in North Philadelphia the evening in question.

A few days later, when both sides rested, the judge gave the jury the case to reach a verdict.

On June 8, 1993, the jury returned a unanimous verdict, finding me guilty of first-degree murder, rape, burglary, robbery, and possession of an instrument of crime.

My family broke down in tears. I felt hopeless and frozen, yet I wanted to console and help them more than I wanted to help myself. The judge banged his gavel for quiet. Attorney Siegel put his head down. I felt finished. Defeated. The Commonwealth of Pennsylvania and the whole Philadelphia Homicide Division were against me.

I went back to my cell that night and thought about everything that I'd been through in my life: my son losing a father, my parents losing a son, my brothers losing a brother, Lisa losing her baby's father to the system. I was possibly to be executed by the State of Pennsylvania for a crime I had nothing to do with. Of course, any hopes of a professional football career were gone now. How could the cops, and the district attorney do this to little ol' me? A young, poor, and Black guy, from the ghetto parts of North Philadelphia. What did I do to deserve this? What had my family and my son done to deserve this? What happened to all those detectives' consciences when they got up on the witness stand and swore to tell the truth in a court of law, to a judge, jury, and the public but told lie after lie, when they forged state documents and committed the crime of absolute perjury one by one? How many other young innocent people from the ghetto did they frame like me? I wondered. Would the truth come out before I was given a possible death sentence? Or was old prison guard Henry right and the battery acid cocktail was on its way right for my innocent veins? Never thought big Anthony "Bolo" Wright from North Philly would go out like this. *Allah, God, if you can hear me up there, I need you on this one.*

CHAPTER 6

I awoke to a loud noise. It was a flashlight sliding across the outside of my cell bars. Then I heard, "Wake up, convicted rapist!" Old prison guard Henry whispered. "That battery acid cocktail is going to have your body jerking once it gets up in your veins, fool."

I jumped up to see the old man taunting me now with his tongue, wiggling it back and forth, mimicking convulsions after being injected.

"I'm gonna get you!" I yelled and went to pop my cell open.

Old Henry took off down the long block, never for me to see him again.

Later, two new prison guards escorted me to the chow hall and then the receiving room.

Today was a new day, I thought, as the bus made its way out of the prison and for the courthouse. The only thing was now, I was a convicted rapist and murderer, and that is a hard pill to swallow when you're an innocent man.

When I arrived at the courthouse, I was informed that I had an attorney visit.

I was escorted to the visiting booth, where I saw Attorney Siegel. Mr. Siegel apologized for the guilty verdict and further explained that the only way I could receive a death sentence was all twelve jurors to unanimously vote for it. He then laid out his strategy for avoiding the death sentence. Then he gave me a brief lecture. "Anthony, they will assert to the jury to kill you. They'll say things like, 'He showed Mrs. Talley no mercy. She fought back, old age and all, and he kept on stabbing her repeatedly until she took her last breath. He made it so personal, so show him no mercy. Vote for death. Death! Death!' No matter what he says, I want you to keep your composure. The worst thing you can do is make any loud outbursts. One defendant jumped up and told the jury, 'Yeah, I did everything he said, but I was only a product of my environment.' The jury gave him death. So, we don't want any of that."

About forty-five minutes later, Mr. Siegel called my mom to the witness stand, followed by my dad. They spoke of my childhood, my football accomplishments, and my being a great dad and made pleas to the jury not to execute their child.

Next, the state's attorney asserted to the jury that they should all vote for the maximum sentence under the law, death, that I was a drug addict, and that I raped Mrs. Talley viciously, stabbed her to death in her own home, and stole her property to support my drug addiction. I wanted to get up and say that these were all lies, propaganda, but I just shook my head in disbelief as I watched him jump around, swing his arms around, and perform for the jury.

Afterward, Mr. Siegel asserted to the jury that Mrs. Talley died a horrible death, but no sentence could bring her back, that I had expressed remorse regarding her death, that I was a young man and a father, and that I would pay for the crime of which they convicted me for the rest of my life in prison. He argued that these mitigating factors outweighed any aggravating circumstances.

Next, the judge instructed the jury to do its job and come back with a penalty verdict. I watched the jurors carefully, trying to see if I could somehow read their thoughts.

My family, sitting behind me, had a look in their eyes that I had never quite seen before, absolute fear.

While waiting for the jury's decision, I said a prayer. I asked Allah to spare my life and to give my family and friends the strength to endure the outcome of this nightmare, continue to maintain their belief in my innocence, and stick by me to overturn this wrongful conviction.

From what I sensed from Mr. Siegel, he was not sure whether he convinced the jury to spare me the death penalty, and that did not make matters any better.

About four hours later, I heard a prison guard's voice. "Wright, you're up. The jury has made their decision."

I rose from the bullpen seat and swallowed hard. This was it, the decision of life or death from the state. I began to think, as the guard escorted me to the elevator, *How did I get here?* Out of all the places in the world, the chances of someone being nearly sentenced to death for a crime he did not commit was less than getting hit by lightning.

There was silence in the courtroom when I arrived. I took a seat beside Mr. Siegel, who avoided any eye contact with me.

"Bailiff, please bring the jury in," the judge announced.

When the jury came in, I noticed some were crying; others remained stone-faced. I did not know how to read this, but my body went numb, as if I were about to be stuck with a needle right then. I looked up at Allah and then closed my eyes and held my breath.

"Ladies and gentlemen of the jury, have you come to a decision?" the judge asked.

"Your Honor, we have not, and we cannot come to a unanimous decision," the foreman advised.

The judge looked a bit disappointed, as if it were a no-brainer. It had been evident that he was in favor of the prosecution.

"Okay, well Juror One, what is your decision?"

"Death, Your Honor."

"Juror Number Two, what is your decision?"

"Death, Judge."

When the judge completed his polling of the jury, it was seven to five in favor of death.

"Yes!" I heard someone behind me blurt out, and I let out the long breath I had been holding. I was relieved.

On the other side of the aisle behind, I began to hear sobbing.

"Order!" the judge shouted, after knocking his gavel. "Ladies and gentlemen of the jury, thank you for your service and all the time you took out of your daily lives to complete your jury duty."

Afterward, the jury disappeared. The state addressed the court, followed by Mr. Siegel.

"Now, the defendant must rise. Mr. Wright, would you like to address the court?"

"Yes, Your Honor. I am an innocent man. My heart goes out to

Mrs. Talley's family. But I am not Mrs. Talley's killer. He is still out there somewhere. I was set up and framed by the police department. I pray that one day the truth comes out, and my name is cleared. I will continue to fight this, until that day comes. I shall overcome. To my family and friends here, please, whatever you do, don't count me out." I turned around to face my family.

Some were crying because I had been convicted, and others looked relieved that my life had just been spared.

"Mr. Wright, if it were left up to me today, I would have sentenced you to death for the horrible crime that you have been convicted of. You claim you're innocent and then have the audacity to blame the fine police department for setting you up, as if it were a big conspiracy to frame you, Mr. Wright, out of the million plus people in the city for this cowardly murder. So, I now sentence you to the custody of the Department of Corrections for a term of life without parole."

All my family now began to cry, as the bailiffs handcuffed me from behind and escorted me out of the courtroom.

The feeling of hearing a judge sentence you to life in prison for a crime you did not commit is indescribable.

CHAPTER 7

The fight was really on now. My main concern after my conviction was overturning it and clearing my name. My case was all over the local television stations. It was also in the *Daily News* and in the *Philadelphia Inquirer* newspaper and other publications. I was sick about it. It was a complete lie, and that hurt like hell.

After my conviction, there were whispers by the bailiffs, prison guards, other prison staff, and the prisoners whenever I came around. I, however, could not let it destroy my sanity or my will to fight because I knew that I did not rape or kill anyone.

Once I was sentenced, my next stop was Graterford State Prison. Graterford, coined, "Grater World" was a bigger version of the Bird, located in Collegeville, Pennsylvania, about forty-five minutes outside of Philadelphia. When I arrived at the castle-like structure, the place was just getting off lockdown for a major geographical gang war.

The major distinction I quickly realized was, unlike the Bird, Graterford housed both Pennsylvania's death row unit and the biggest prison population of the state, many of whom were lifers. It was the mecca of the Pennsylvania prison system and therefore the best place to do your time in the state. All the state senators, state representatives, and city councilmen visited the prison to politic with the men and speak of their new bills. The mayor and various organizations also came to visit regularly. Lawyers held seminars, and there was a Lifer's Organization and NAACP and Gray Panther chapters that helped Graterford residents cope with their sentences and various other prison street matters.

The prison yard was huge. There was a line of handball courts and basketball courts, weights, and pull-up bars, and in the middle of the yard was the diamond-shaped baseball field, which was surrounded by a running track. Graterford also had a football team, a baseball team, and boxing tournaments for the inmates, which instantly piqued my interest. I also noticed that just about everyone had a hustle, and if you didn't, you had best to get one. There were a variety of jobs in the prison that consisted of block janitors, block clerks, block cable representatives, kitchen workers, laundry workers, shoe shop workers, and commissary workers, all of which generally started at nineteen cents an hour. I said to my neighbor, "What you mean, nineteen cent an hour?"

He replied, "It's slave wages, man. Read the Thirteenth Amendment, man. Slavery was only partially over."

"The Thirteenth Amendment?" I said.

"Yeah, of the United States Constitution. They got it down there in the law library."

I just smiled. Afterward, he explained that there were higher-paying jobs. The main one was working in the CI shop. There, the Department of Corrections had contracts with the state to make products, like license plates, and paid inmates' lower rates than in society. In 1991, minimum wage was about $3.35 an hour, but an inmate in the CI shop would make up to $300 a month with overtime. That took a guy with no support from home a long way in the penitentiary.

The commissary was Graterford's grocery store, and prices were high. The cost of living was expensive, despite society's view of it.

On the black market, guys made money selling everything from all sorts of sandwiches and food products taken from the prison's kitchen to hand-drawn greeting cards, oils and incense, new underclothes, and services like sewing and hemming clothes, and, of course, there were drugs of all sorts and knives being sold as well.

Most of the guards were Black, cool, and from Philadelphia. The main thing that the guards' superiors concerned them with was "count." When I arrived at Graterford in 1991, there were three counts; that meant you had to be in your cell (or someone who could pass for you did) when the guards came around to count your body. After they called in the count, if it cleared, your door popped open, and it was on. If count did not clear, it meant somebody couldn't count, and they would have to do it all over again until the count was cleared.

A few days after my arrival, I called home and learned that my family was being harassed and shunned. My mom's so-called friends had disassociated themselves from her after they had learned about my conviction from the media. When the word had hit the streets, even the young kids were taunting my family members. That hurt more than anything. I knew I had to remain focused on appealing the conviction to the Pennsylvania superior court. Mr. Siegel said after my sentencing that he would appeal, but I was hesitant because I was not confident that he could get me the success and results I needed.

Once I got settled in, I scheduled a visit to the law library. I knew if I would be successful in clearing my name and overturning this conviction, I had to educate myself better with this law. Although I kept to myself for the most part, the old heads from my neighborhood, Oxford Street in North Philly, showed me around. When a new arrival came through from the neighborhood, a crew would show him the ropes. From the beginning, I made it known that I was innocent of the rape and murder crime that I was sure they had heard about. Some from the neighborhood welcomed me, while others kept their distance. I was okay with that as long as they didn't disrespect me. Others did not care; they just wanted me on their football team, to play the running back position. Though Graterford held many lifers, the majority had time in, had changed their lives, were laid back, and ran the prison. Many of the young bucks were lost, wild, and needed guidance from the old heads. I was only twenty years old, in a jungle, left to die. But I had other plans.

CHAPTER 8

Before I knew it, a year had nearly passed at Graterford. Because I could not afford counsel for the appeal, I ended up using a court-appointed attorney. The superior court denied all our issues about a year later. Attorney Siegel did not file a petition for allowance of appeal to the Pennsylvania Supreme Court or my federal claims of innocence to the federal court, which were my next appeal steps. I felt Attorney Siegel had left me for dead. I fell into a deep depression, and I did not want to be bothered with anyone. I still couldn't come to grips with being convicted of this horrible rape and murder of the elderly Mrs. Talley. Although I did not viciously stab her to death like I was convicted of doing, I felt sorry for her, and I had nightmares of what she must have gone through and how much pain she suffered when he stabbed her to death. "Why me?" I asked daily when I awoke to the confines of a Graterford prison cell.

Soon, I felt myself becoming somewhat antisocial and drained. Yet in my heart, I knew I still had to fight. In August of 1996, I hustled up some packs of Newport cigarettes and paid a jailhouse lawyer to file my postconviction relief petition. In Pennsylvania, all defendants are entitled to appointed counsel on their first postconviction petition.

So, after my petition was initiated, the court appointed me a young attorney from the Philadelphia public defender's office, whose name I have already forgotten, but let me name him Attorney Young. He never visited me so I could aid him in my defense or to see if I had any new evidence that could help in my appeal. I only knew he was appointed to the case after I wrote to the clerk for my docket statement sheet that showed all the case activity. Because his office did not accept collect calls, I had to go through a lot of changes to get my unit counselor, Mrs. Burks, to give me a free direct call to him.

After the last of three attempts to contact him, Mrs. Burks caught him.

"Hello, is this Attorney Young?" I asked.

"Yes, who's this?" he replied with an attitude.

"It's Anthony Wright. The court appointed you to represent me on my PCRA."

"Anthony Wright? It doesn't ring a bell."

"You should've received a copy of the court order and my petition."

"You know how many court orders I get? Hold on!"

Mrs. Burks could hear the conversation. She looked at me and shrugged her shoulders.

"Yeah, I know who you are," he said when he came back on the line. "What can I do for you?"

"I wanted to talk to you in person about my claims of innocence."

"I read this file over; it's no need. I don't see any merits in your claims."

"What do you mean? I am innocent!" I stressed.

"Yeah, you and the whole Graterford. Do you have any idea how many times I hear that a day? I don't have the time. I'm about to step out for lunch—" *Click!* He had hung up on me, leaving me beyond stunned.

"Tony, see you put me through all of this to call this guy, and what did he tell you? Nothing!"

A few months later, I had to hustle up some Newport cigarettes to pay the jailhouse lawyer to file my petition because Public Defender Young refused to and would not accept my calls. He also hung up on my mother when she said she was calling on my behalf. The postconviction petition was denied by the court with little justification. At this point, I was fed up of the courts denying me an opportunity to prove my innocence. How could this happen in America? The realization began to settle in that I might not make it out of prison alive. But I promised myself that I would not stop fighting.

Soon I got with an older guy in the law library named Ameen. He said there was another way I could possibly get out, and that was filing for commutation. He told me to sign up for the law library, and he would go over my case. I signed up and eagerly waited to be scheduled. The next day, I received a visit from Momma Marilyn. Although she had visited regularly in the last year and brought Anthony Jr., on this day, she arrived alone. After we embraced and took a seat, I knew something was wrong.

"What is it, Mom?" I asked with concern.

"It's Lisa," she said with tears filling up her eyes. "She ain't doing well."

"What do you mean, Mom?"

"Tony, she is messing with that stuff."

"What stuff, Mom?" I asked. Though I sensed where she was going, I just wanted to be sure.

"Crack, Tony. She is hitting the pipe!" As I took the information in, I was lost for words. "Tony," Mom went on, "she has been so stressed about you, Tony Jr., and about life. I began noticing strange behavior. Then I caught her one night when I came downstairs to get something to drink from the refrigerator. She and other women that I never seen before were sitting out on the porch, just smoking up a storm from the pipe. I couldn't believe my eyes. Then it all made sense."

"Wow, Mom … I'm really sorry to hear this."

"I don't want little Tony around that nonsense, so I told her she had to leave. So now she's out there on the streets, doing God knows what to support her habit."

After the visit, I went back to the cell. I was crushed. My child's mom had fallen victim to the crack epidemic. That explained why she never brought our son to come see me and why she wasn't answering my calls. She was hitting the pipe. I wanted to help her, but now, I couldn't even help myself. I was in the penitentiary with a life sentence.

CHAPTER 9

When I arrived at the law library, Ameen was seated with a spot reserved for me. He waved me over, and I joined him with my case file. He looked eager to help me. He was in his late forties, tall, and dark-skinned. He wore wire-framed glasses and was educated in law. Many came to him for legal assistance because he was a lifer with about twenty years in prison and had gotten two men released. His mood changed when he began reading my case file.

"I have to be up front with you, Tony," he said after completing my file. "I've filed many commutations for guys, and in Pennsylvania, they generally only grant it for the accomplices in murder cases."

"What about if you didn't do it at all?" I asked with disappointment.

"That's the thing, Tony: you must make that crystal clear to them, but they don't review your case like a judge or jury would for innocence or guilt. They presume that the jury or judge got it right and that you are in fact guilty but should be granted another chance because you played a minor role in the offense. In your case, you are the principal and sole defendant, so honestly, I don't think they'd ever grant you commutation."

It was not a good feeling hearing those words in what may have been my only other way out of prison alive.

"Tony, if you're saying you didn't do this, then you got to focus on the DNA, man, to prove your innocence," Ameen said as he looked me in the eye.

I could see that Ameen was skeptical about whether I was innocent. There was doubt of my innocence in his tone and manner, as there had been with Attorney Siegel and Public Defender Young. I was used to it by then. Most people with legal minds all assumed that I was guilty after reviewing the pieces of fabricated evidence the detectives put together against me. I felt doomed when I thought that even my fellow prisoners assumed that the police would not just set a man up with all this evidence if he was not indeed guilty. I knew I had a hard battle ahead of me.

Damn, they got me good, I thought.

"I think you should write the Innocence Project. If they think you're innocent, they may take your case. Here's their address." Ameen passed me a piece of paper. I went back to my cell and immediately began writing the Innocence Project. After that, I began collecting extra pens, paper, and envelopes from other prisoners to start a writing campaign. I wrote ten letters a day, seven days a week, to anyone I thought might give a damn. To take my mind off my seemingly doomed sentence, I began to work my body like a machine. I would lift weights three times a day, six days a week, and soon the guys from Oxford Street began calling me "the Bolo Machine." I also played sports regularly and took a job as a referee. I figured if I stayed busy, I would be too busy to really feel the pain and torture of being an innocent man in prison for life. But how wrong I was.

CHAPTER 10

Marilyn Martin was one of nine kids by Mary and Caesar Wright who were raised in Philadelphia. My mom got pregnant with me in 1970 by a neighborhood boy named David Parker. They weren't a couple when I was born in 1971. My dad moved down to Georgia in 1979, and he would fly me down each summer and Christmas to spend time with him. Later, Momma Marilyn married a man named William Martin, and we moved in with her mother-in-law. William drank regularly, and Mom began to drink with him. After some time passed, the relationship ran its course. Mom later met a man named Harry. He ran a speakeasy in the Nicetown section of the city. He pulled in plenty of money, dressed Momma Marilyn and me in expensive clothes, and drove us around the neighborhood in his new Cadillac. But when Harry got drunk, he would whip me for the smallest things.

When he began to beat Momma Marilyn, I stepped up and was told I had to leave. So, I stayed with family and friends. Eventually, I got left behind in school because I was never in one place long and dropped out at sixteen. Next, I began hanging out with the corner boys, which would lead to trouble. The best thing my mom did for me at this point I recall is when I went back down south to spend time with my dad, and he got me enrolled in the Organized Football League.

"Mr. Wright, they want you down at the chapel to see the imam," a prison guard said, snapping me out of my daydream. "Here's your pass," he continued and then walked down the tier.

I slipped on my brown issued clothes, wishing I could step back in time. Although I had had a tough childhood, things seemed much simpler then.

I had not seen Imam Tahier in some time, and I wondered why he had summoned me to his office as I walked down the tier. Although I had not been attending Jumah regularly, I was still listed as a Sunni Muslim. I had taken my Shahadah (to testify that there is no deity worthy of worship but Allah, and Muhammad is the messenger of Allah) in the eighties. I was not a religious fanatic, but I believed in God and his prophets. When I arrived at the chapel, Imam Tahier escorted me into his office and showed me a chair. He was a short and slim African man who appeared to be in his forties. He was polite, friendly, and always smelled of sandalwood and frankincense oil fragrances.

"How have you been, Anthony?" Imam Tahier said as he took a seat at his desk.

"I'm hanging in there, Imam. How about you?" I said, scanning his neat office and the Islamic books lined on his shelf.

"I'm doing well. I called you here today unfortunately to inform you, Tony, that your mother has slipped into a diabetic coma, and they have her in the hospital on life support."

I just stared at the imam, dumbfounded. Visions of her rocking me to sleep when I was a young boy flashed in my mind. Then there was she and I going to get ice cream on Saturday afternoon. Then suddenly, I thought of our last visit together, our last embrace.

"Tony, I'm really sorry," Imam Tahier said, snapping me out of my reverie.

"Are you sure she's in a coma?" I managed to murmur.

"Yes, Tony. I spoke with your aunt Gladys Brown."

Aunt Gladys was the oldest of my mother's siblings. She had worked with the Department of Veterans Affairs for forty-two years before she retired and was the organizer who kept the family together. My eyes filled up with tears.

"Would you like to speak to her?"

I nodded. When Aunt Gladys answered, I instantly knew it was true. I could hear it all in her voice. I also heard hollering in the background.

"Tony ... it doesn't look good," she cried. "She's in a diabetic coma, and the doctor said her condition is worsening." In a saddened voice, she said, "Her body is beginning to swell."

"What can he do for her?" I asked with more concern.

"The doctor said ... not much. And since you are the only son, we are requesting that you be brought down here to make the decision."

But the courts would never let me go to the hospital to see about my mother. They didn't care. I'd grown to know that the system was heartless. They had stopped me from seeing the very woman who had pushed me into this world, the same world that had shown me so much heartache, pain, and despair. Visions of her begging the jury not to kill her only son played repeatedly in my mind. She had fought for me when I needed her most. Now I couldn't even do the same for her.

When I broke the news to my aunt Gladys, she threw a fit. "Them folks is gonna pay one day, because God don't like ugly. They put us through all this bull for something you ain't even do, and now they won't even let you see your momma."

Chapter 11

In the last few weeks, Imam Tahier summoned me to the chapel on several occasions. When he called for me on this day, however, something felt different. When I arrived, the imam could not even look me in the eye as he met me at the chapel door and asked me to follow him to his office. Once there, he asked me to take a seat and then closed the door behind us.

"Tony, I got a call from your aunt Gladys a little while ago. Unfortunately, your mom is no longer on life support. This afternoon, she passed, Tony."

I knew this day was coming, and I thought I had prepared myself for it, but when I heard the words come out of his mouth, I was not ready at all. Slowly, it all began to sink in. I lowered my head in grief.

"I'm sorry, Tony. Allah willing, she will rest in peace."

I nodded.

"Let me put you through to your dad," Imam Tahier insisted.

"Tony, I pray that she is in a better place now," my dad said.

"This is tough, Dad."

After we spoke for a short while, I headed back to my cell with thoughts of our great loss. I instantly realized nothing can prepare a person for the feelings that comes with losing the person who pushed you into this world. When I arrived on my unit, I did not want to be bothered with anyone. I headed directly to my cell. It was times like this that I was fortunate to be in a single-man cell. I was not in a mood to be social. If it weren't for Momma Marilyn, there was no way I could have survived and maintained my sanity in a madhouse like Graterford State Prison as long as I did. I lay on the bed in deep thought. Although I had been introduced to Islam before I landed at Graterford, I never offered prayer to Allah (God). Soon, I got up and looked out the window. It began to rain. I got down on my knees and offered a prayer. I cried out to God and asked why he took Momma Marilyn from me when he knew she was all I really had, and I was stuck in prison to die for a crime I did not commit. To make matters worse, the prison not only denied me a visit to my mom in the hospital under supervision, but I was also denied attending the funeral to pay my respects.

The day of her funeral, I sat in my cell grieving her loss. In the afternoon, a prison guard slipped an envelope into my cell while doing his mail delivery tour. I got up and retrieved the envelope. It was from the Innocence Project, which piqued my interest. I tore the envelope open with excitement. The letter read:

> Mr. Wright, we are writing to inform you that we received your request for our office to review your case for possible acceptance for us to aid in the litigation of your case. After careful review of your case, we believe in your innocence, and we have accepted your case to fight for you.

I jumped for joy after receiving the news. I was so overwhelmed with so many emotions that I began to pace. Then, I decided to go out on the block to call my dad back.

"Hello?" he answered in a low tone.

"Hey, Dad, I just got a letter from the Innocence Project, saying they have accepted my case and that they believe in my innocence."

"Oh, Tony, that is great news, Son. Your mother, Tony, it's your mother. She's up there with God now, and I can feel that. She asked him to help, said 'My son needs help down there!' It's no coincidence that a few days after she leaves us, and on the day of her funeral, you receive this important mail that we have waited so long for."

We both broke down after that. Momma Marilyn would always be in my thoughts. After speaking to my dad, I learned that Lisa did not attend my mother's funeral. I can't say that I was a bit surprised because many kept me informed of her erratic behavior since succumbing to the crack epidemic. I knew with her never bringing Tony Jr. to come to see me at Graterford, my relationship with my son would suffer a big blow. Hopefully, I thought, with the Innocence Project on board now, it wouldn't be long before I could reunite with my son and the rest of my family. Thing was, when dealing with the court and the prison system, I knew that it would be a fought fight.

CHAPTER 12

On September 9, 2001, the Pennsylvania Legislature enacted DNA testing for prisoners claiming innocence under Section 9543.1. Attorney Nina Morrison from the Innocence Project came to visit me. She was a smart and pretty Latino lawyer with a strong passion for justice and worked with the attorneys from the Innocence Project of Brandies University in New York. She said we would be filing a petition under the new statute for DNA testing to prove my innocence. I was very excited after seeing her, and it gave me hope again that I would get out. I knew if I could get the testing done, it would exonerate me once it came back. I also couldn't wait to see whom the DNA actually identified. The real killer was not only still out there, but he had ruined my entire life.

"The problem now is getting the court to let us do the testing," I said, concerned.

"There's no reason, Tony, the court should deny this petition under this new statute. This is what this bill was put in place for," Attorney Morrison replied.

A Philadelphia attorney named Sondra Rodriguez also came on board, pro bono (free of charge). Later, they filed a petition to the court under the 9543.1 statute, asserting that I was innocent of the rape and murder of Mrs. Talley. We requested a form of more advanced DNA testing known as short tandem repeat ("STR") analysis, which we asserted was not available during my first trial. STR testing became available in 1999. It is statistically improbable for any two random individuals in the world, except identical twins, to share the same DNA profile obtained from this test. We further argued that such testing could demonstrate my actual innocence, and we requested the PCRA court to grant us permission to test the semen and bloodstains found on the jeans, the fitted sheet taken from Mrs. Talley's bed, the bloodstains on the sweatshirt, the handle of the kitchen knife, and the oral, vaginal, and rectal swabs taken during Mrs. Talley's autopsy. We also asserted that if tested that the results could be entered into the national DNA database for the purpose of finding the actual individual who committed the crimes.

On July 10, 2006, Philadelphia Common Pleas Judge, the Honorable D. Webster Keogh denied our motion for testing. I was crushed, as were my attorneys and supporters. In Judge Keogh's opinion, he focused on my confession and ruled that because I signed the confession prepared by the cops, that I was not entitled to obtain DNA testing to prove my innocence.

Attorney Morrison was back up to see me, and she was furious. "This ruling is horrible!" she shouted. "It's not supported by the law that is similar to the facts in this case, and we are definitely appealing this, Tony. You just hang in there, you hear me?"

"Yeah, I will hang in there. I mean, I have this long, why not a couple more years?" I said, more depressed the more I thought about it. "How could the court rule like this? Those corrupt cops framing me, drafting up a confession, and then threatening me to sign it has nothing to do with the DNA showing the real killer is still out there!"

"I know, Tony. The judge seized upon the loophole in the bill that states a court 'shall not order DNA testing if, after review of the record, the court determines there is no reasonable possibility that the testing would produce exculpatory evidence that would establish … actual innocence.' He wrote in his opinion, 'there is no such reasonable possibility in this case,'" she said, quoting the court's ruling. "Believe me, it's a terrible ruling." She looked into my eyes. "It's rulings like this that make people give up on the justice system. The point of this bill was to test convictions just like yours. To get to the truth. DNA don't lie. And we intend to prove that. One way or another."

I was struck by her determination to fight the system. "We will appeal the decision, Tony. We know how important getting this DNA test is to you."

"Yeah. It's a matter of life or death."

CHAPTER 13

A longtime friend named Darnell Fischer stepped up after my mother's death. He would bring Anthony Jr. up to Graterford to see me at least once a month, and he would send me money to buy groceries in the prison commissary and to pay my medical and cable fees. The tension of being confined, oppressed, and forgotten becomes so great at times, in order to maintain your sanity, you need to take your mind off your reality. TV and radio can be this stress reliever. Others turned to drugs, alcohol, tobacco, caffeine, violence, sex, and gambling. Unlike prisons in other states, in Pennsylvania, a prisoner had to pay for cable if he wanted to watch TV, and the cost was regularly increased. I would regularly read articles in the newspaper on negative views regarding cable availability in prison. But many people in charge realized that it was smart to keep prisoners occupied. It would help prevent creating a hostile and unsafe environment for both staff and the prison residents.

Many of the so-called prison luxury critics also apparently failed to recognize that there were actually a lot of people in prison who were innocent, and we were suffering daily from not only a loss of freedom and liberty but our pursuit of happiness, companionship, and a list of other humanly things as well. I was young when I came to prison, and

I had a desire to settle down with a woman and create a family. The chances of achieving that desire seemed slim at times, especially with the constant appeal denials from the courts.

A friend named Charmaine was a longtime supporter. She did not judge me and believed in my innocence, when so many other so-called friends bit my back out and turned their backs on me. She would come up to Graterford to visit and run small errands for me in the city. Long-term romantic relationships were difficult to keep or maintain in the Pennsylvania prison system. Unlike prisons in New York, Connecticut, California, and other states, there were no conjugal visits in the state of Pennsylvania. Though conjugal visits were a goal to fight for for the Lifer's Organization in the Pennsylvania prison system, the fight did not make much progress. But prisoners who came down from New York and other states with Pennsylvania detainers stated that the conjugal weekend visits kept families together and maintained marriages and relationships for guys and girls returning to the communities. In fact, a few guys who had come down to Graterford from other states complained that their marriages had greatly suffered, and some ended, as their spouses and family could not function the same without those weekend conjugal visits.

In 1989, a riot broke out in a Pennsylvania prison called "Camp Hill." Many of those prisoners were transferred to Graterford and explained that they got fed up with the oppressive and abusive conditions of the prison, as well as the lack of professionalism and rehabilitation. Others who were released were mentally scarred and sought retribution when released. The Pennsylvania Department of Corrections Code of

Ethics called, without exception, for each employee in the correctional system to subscribe to the principle that something positive can be done for each inmate. The problem was those principles were not adhered to, or enforced, from the top.

The grievance system for prisoners in Pennsylvania was biased and poorly managed by the prison administration, and the statistics showed that over 95 percent of grievances filed by prisoners were decided in the staff's favor. In contrast, over 90 percent of the misconduct reports written by prison staff were upheld against prisoners. This fact only led to more abuse of authority by staff. Attorneys of the Disability Rights Network, Human Rights Coalition, the American Civil Liberties Union, and the Justice Department all had begun investigating the constitutional violations being implemented by the Pennsylvania Department of Corrections' employees and the misuse and overuse of solitary confinement that was causing men and women to hang themselves.

The investigation later led to a class action lawsuit, the *Disability Rights Network of Pennsylvania vs. John Wetzel*, as the secretary of the Pennsylvania Department of Corrections, in the United States District Court for the Middle District of Pennsylvania. Secretary Wetzel later settled the lawsuit and agreed to impose a number of changes to the prison conditions that included some restrictions on the use of solitary confinement. Although I was in agreement with more humane prison conditions and the great need for the improvement of the living conditions in prison, I had to put most of my energy into getting out altogether. I knew guys who filed numerous lawsuits against the prison. They had gotten so caught up in prison politics and became so institutionalized that they did not even appeal the sentence that they had received to be in prison in the first place. I did not want to be that guy.

CHAPTER 14

I had developed a good rapport with a sergeant at Graterford, whom I will call Officer Brown. Officer Brown was a Black woman from North Philadelphia. What I appreciate about Officer Brown was she understood the struggle from her upbringing. I had watched her over the years, and she never oppressed others, abused her authority, or spoke down to others like many of her coworkers. Rather she always used her position to help others and defuse an incident before it blew up and out of control. I witnessed some of the female guests of Graterford act and speak more aggressively than men.

One female officer spoke to a young guy out of South Philly like a dog. Their troubles only escalated, and he warned her, "You keep talking to me like a man, I'm going treat you like a man."

The next morning, guards' keys began jiggling as they ran to assist the young female officer, who had been knocked out by the young guy from South Philly. Although the young officer had abused her authority and had provoked the kid, I couldn't stand to see a man hit a woman. After all that had been done, Sergeant Brown did not condone the guards beating the young dude down after he was put in restraints. She said the hearing examiner and the judge would take care of him, after he was charged with assaulting the female officer. Shortly after, she came to my cell after she had gone to lunch. I immediately sensed that something was not the same. She was acting very distant and not her usual self.

"What's wrong?" I asked as she stood in front of my cell.

"Why you say that?" she responded, not giving me any eye contact.

"The way you are acting. You barely spoke to me in the last few days, and you can't even look me in the eyes all of sudden."

"Well, I'm not gonna lie; I did hear something about you."

"What you hear?" I said with curiosity.

"Someone said, 'Why you always talking to that convicted rapist?' referring to you."

"Oh yeah, well, I ain't no rapist!"

"Look, I ain't here to judge nobody, but are you saying you ain't do it?"

"Yeah, that's exactly what I'm saying. I was framed by the Philadelphia Police Department."

"Really?" she asked, looking at me skeptically.

"Ms. Brown, I know it may seem farfetched, but it's true, and I have no reason to lie to you. Take a look at this," I said and retrieved the Innocence Project's case acceptance letter from off the top of my cabinet.

She examined the letter, and I watched her closely as she took it all in.

"They went over my case very thoroughly. Do you think they

would've took my case on if they thought I was really a rapist or that I murdered the victim?"

"Tony, listen, thanks for sharing this with me, but like I said, I'm not here to judge you. Was I troubled about your case once I heard about it? Yes. But honestly, after getting to know you over the years, you don't strike me as someone that could've done something like this to an elderly woman."

"Because I didn't! And I want to know who told you that!"

"I'm not going to tell you that, Tony, because I don't want you getting into no trouble. You have enough to worry about."

"You don't think that I have a right to know?"

"Yes, but under the circumstances, I can't tell you. Now, what I will do is check the person and let it be known that they don't know all the facts of your case, and they should be worried about their own. Because if they said that to me, they probably said it to someone else."

Later that night, my conversation with Ms. Brown played back in my mind over and over again. There's no other feeling in the world like being falsely accused of something of this magnitude and to have people thinking you did it, when all along, you know you didn't. Although it was eating me up inside that the court had denied my DNA testing, I knew I would never give up hope or my willpower to show the world that I was an innocent man.

CHAPTER 15

"Anthony Wright, visit!" I heard come over the block speakers.

After going through a brief search, I walked out to the visiting room to see Attorney Morrison standing with her briefcase. I shook her hand, and we took a seat.

"I was surprised when they called me for a visit."

"Yes, I know you wasn't expecting me, Tony, but I wanted to come up to tell you in person that we got a decision from the Supreme Court about your petition. I have it right here with me," she said, opening her briefcase and producing the court's decision. "We won, Tony!" she said excitedly. "Yes, we won!"

"That's really good news, Ms. Morrison," I said, shaking my head in disbelief. "The hard work paid off," I said, letting out a deep breath, and leaned back in my chair.

"Yes. So now, we can make arrangements for you to take the test."

"Okay. I'm ready."

"We will be contacting the state attorney's office, so we can come up with a fair process, to ensure it does not get tampered with."

"For sure. I know they are not happy about this."

"You're right about that. You know, I was talking to my colleagues about you yesterday. You sit here excited now, but you have remained so calm for all these years. We know that you were framed by the Philadelphia Police Department, and that has to be just about the most horrendous thing that can happen to someone."

"It is. I think about that all the time. I used to think that getting framed by the police was as rare as someone getting struck by lightning until it happened to me."

"Wow, that is something, Tony."

"Yeah, it is."

"What kept you going all these years?"

"My mother, my family. I couldn't give up. I know I had to keep fighting for this very day. 'Cause you know what? That test is gonna show that the real killer is still out there somewhere, or he is dead. But most importantly, it's gonna show that I'm innocent."

Attorney Morrison stared as her eyes filled with tears. That night, I called my dad to share the good news. He was so excited he began to cry and get emotional. I knew that he had faith that the test would come back exonerating me of this vicious crime that the state of Pennsylvania tried to put me to death for and had me sentenced to life in prison for. So, as far as I was concerned, the test could not come soon enough.

"Tony, I was instructed to provide you with a legal call," Counsel Burk said as I stood in front of my block.

I followed her into her office, and she called Attorney Morrison for me.

"Hello?"

"Tony, we got the test results, and it's not good at all. It shows that you are the donor of the DNA on the crime scene. We had so much faith in you. How could you waste our time?"

"It's got to be wrong. They tampered with it! I promise you, it was not me. They had to get to it!" I yelled into the receiver.

Suddenly, I was awakened by the 6:00 a.m. count bell. I looked around and realized that it was a nightmare. It had to be my subconscious talking because I was paranoid about the test somehow being tampered with. I would have been a fool not to feel that way. They had done it before, so nothing made me feel that they wouldn't try again. After count, I jumped back in the bed and tossed and turned for about an hour. I could not sleep. About an hour later, a guard knocked on my cell door. "Mr. Wright, they want you in the visiting area."

It was time. This was it—one of the most important tests in my life. I walked to the visiting room, and the guard there told me that somebody was there to see me. About ten minutes later, a tall, white male came through the door. He introduced himself as Barry Reynolds, an independent forensic analyst who was approved by the court to conduct my DNA test. I was happy to hear he was approved by the court, but I was still concerned about where my DNA would end up after he left. I watched him closely as he removed a kit from a black bag.

After he swabbed my mouth with a number of Q-tips and placed them in a bag. I watched him closely seal them. I knew this was the key to my freedom.

CHAPTER 16

A week went by, and I had so much on my mind. Word had gotten around the jail that the DNA test had exonerated me. All the ones who had had my back out and seemed to believe that I was what the state tried to make me out to be—a cold-blooded rapist and murderer—had a "new attitude" like Patty LaBelle would say. I, however, didn't need any new friends, especially ones who sided with the state, so I stuck with my normal crew: Big Gee, Marshall, Blue, and Benny Gage.

I would play handball on the weekends with my crew to get a good sweat, and I maintained a hard workout routine that would put a pro athlete on his back.

My crew took care of me. When I didn't have it, they were there for me. We would bid hard, but the truth was I was tired. I really wanted to go home. After all, I was an innocent man all along, and there's but so much you can take.

The next day, a high-ranking SCI Huntingdon staff member, Major Scottie Walters, came to see me.

"Bolo, how do you feel?" Major Walters asked. He always called me by my nickname.

"I feel good," I replied.

"Heard the news, and you know what? I ain't a bit surprised. I read your file when you first got here, and you know what? I watched you. I mean I watched you when you didn't even know I was watching."

"Yeah, I get it. It's cameras all around this place."

"My case in point, so after a while of watching, I said to myself, something ain't right here. There's no way this guy did what they have accused him of and got some jury to convict him of it."

"I've always been innocent, but after a while, you just get tired of saying it. And you want to prove it. And hopefully now I have."

"I believe you did. I told my wife that. Well, good luck to you. Are you ready for your visit?"

"What visit?"

"I just heard them call you on my walkie. It's your lawyer girl. Hopefully you're out of here."

"Yeah, I hope."

I got my pass from the block guard and headed to my visit. When I got there, Attorney Morrison was seated. However, unlike our last visit, she did not have that same spark, so I sensed something was up.

"Good afternoon, Tony."

"How are you? Thanks for coming."

"Well, as promised, I told you when I heard something, you'd hear something."

"Right."

"Attorney Nuefeld and I had a meeting with District Attorney Seth Williams and his assistant yesterday."

"Okay," I replied. I was all ears.

"They conceded that the DNA exonerated you of raping and killing the victim, but their position now is witnesses put you on the scene, so you must have been the accomplice."

"Accomplice?" I exploded and rose from my chair. Other visitors looked our way.

"I know, Tony. Please sit. Trust me, I know. The audacity of them. They told the court and a jury you were the rapist killer, tried to give you a lethal injection, and now they say, oh perhaps he was an accomplice of the killer. I could hardly stomach it myself, so I know how you must be feeling."

"Is everything okay?" a potbellied prison guard said, appearing from behind the desk.

"Yes, thank you," Attorney Morrison replied, and the guard walked off. "Tony, I need you to understand that we are on your side."

"I believe that."

"In a nutshell, they are more concerned with the reputation of those crooked detectives that set you up and the entire police department, along with the money the state would have to pay out after they are slapped with a fat lawsuit for all of this that they are still trying to cover up."

"Of course they are."

"And we know damn well, those witnesses they claim that put you on the scene of the crime are the very ones the police coerced into saying it was you to begin with."

"Those are my thoughts exactly."

"Whoa, this is a shame. I need a second." Attorney Morrison exhaled and took a moment to collect her thoughts.

"You okay?" I asked.

"Yeah, I should be the one asking you that."

"It's all good. So, tell me what happens next."

"Okay," Attorney Morrison stated as she regrouped. "What's next is we are putting in a motion to dismiss these convictions based on newly discovered DNA test results that prove that you are actually innocent."

"Okay," I replied, taking it all in.

"Then as an alternative we are asking the court to grant you a new trial based on the newly discovered DNA test results."

"Then what?"

"If we get the dismissal, you walk out of here a free man. If they only grant us a new trial, then guess what."

"What's that?"

"We are gonna tear them a new one."

"Now, you're talking."

"You ready?" she asked, looking me directly in the eye.

"Ready as I ever will be," I replied.

CHAPTER 17

A month later, a prison guard came to my cell.

"Anthony Wright, you got court. You're going ATA," he said, looking in at me, "so be sure to pack up and bring your stuff to the property room."

Two days later, I was at Philadelphia County Jail, CFCF, on State Road. The jail was named after a former Warden Curran and Deputy Warden Fromhold of Holmesburg city jail, which was also on State Road. Both Curran and Fromhold were stabbed to death on May 31, 1973, at Holmesburg by prisoners Joseph "JoJo" Bowen and Fredrick "Muhammad" Burton. The incident occurred when Bowen and Burton attended a meeting with Curran and Fromhold in the warden's office pertaining to the living conditions and restrictions at Holmesburg. Once inside the meeting, the attack began. Both Bowen and Burton were ultimately convicted of the murder and sentenced to life imprisonment. These days, the jail is referred to as CFCF.

During my stay there, it was overcrowded, unorganized, and poorly run. The jail was so overcrowded that they turned all double cells into three-man cells by merely putting an additional mattress on the floor.

They also turned the janitor rooms on the unit into four-man cells. The majority of the staff was from Philadelphia or nearby counties.

By that time, my case was all over the news and in the newspapers, and the staff and jail detainees knew exactly who I was. The next day, I was at the Philadelphia courthouse on Filbert Street. Inside the courtroom, I was seated next to Attorney Nuefeld and Attorney Morrison. Across from us was Assistant District Attorney Tom Evans and Assistant District Attorney Lisa Reynolds. When Judge Michal Fletcher appeared from his chambers, we all rose until he was seated.

"You may be seated," Judge Fletcher instructed. He was an old white-haired man who wore thick, black-framed glasses.

After the judge's clerk read the case number, Judge Fletcher spoke again.

"Good morning. Today we are here on the account of the defendant's motion to dismiss or alternatively grant the defendant a new trial. Before I hear from the defense counsel, are there any other motions or concerns that either party wishes to raise at this time?"

"No, Your Honor." Attorney Nuefeld rose.

"No, Your Honor." Attorney Evans rose.

"You may be seated," Judge Fletcher instructed.

"Very well, Mr. Nuefeld, you may proceed with your motion."

"Thank you, Your Honor. As this court is aware, after this court granted that new DNA testing be conducted in this case, that test proves without a doubt, that Mr. Anthony Wright was not the person responsible for raping or killing Mrs. Talley back in 1991. Based on this newly discovered evidence, we move to have Your Honor grant our motion to dismiss this case or, alternatively, grant Mr. Wright a new trial. First, we would stress to the court that this DNA test exoneration favors a dismissal. Mr. Wright was nearly executed for this crime that evidence shows he did not commit. He has also spent over twenty-four long years in prison for this now. I am also happy to announce today to this court and to my client for the first time, that just yesterday evening, the FBI DNA database made a match to the DNA left at this very crime, and it identifies that individual as Ronnie Byrd."

There was a gasp, followed by murmurs in the courtroom.

"Your Honor," Attorney Nuefeld continued, "I have already provided a certified copy of these results to Mr. Evans. This new evidence shows that Ronnie Byrd is without a doubt Mrs. Talley's Killer and that Mr. Wright is actually innocent and should be released," Attorney Nuefeld closed with passion.

"The state?" Judge Fletcher asked.

"Your Honor," DA Evans rose and began. "The state position is yes, the new DNA test shows that the defendant is not the donor of the semen or items touched by the killer, that is, the weapon. However, this does not let Mr. Wright all the way off the hook as his counsel argues. Two adults and three then teens positively identified the defendant going into the house the evening of Mrs. Talley's death. Therefore, there's still ample evidence that the defendant acted as an accomplice. And as the court knows, under the accomplice liability statute, the defendant would indeed receive a life sentence for that role. So, in essence, the defendant would still end up with life. Therefore, this court should deny the defendant's motion," DA Evans said and then took a seat.

Attorney Nuefeld jumped to his feet. "Your Honor, the state has never charged Mr. Wright as an accomplice. So it's ludicrous for the state to think they can switch up their theory of the case at this late juncture. Moreover, Mr. Wright's due process rights would clearly be violated because he was never timely put on notice that he was being charged as an accomplice."

"All right … all right," Judge Fletcher began. "We will take a lunch recess while I take this under advisement. This court is adjourned until 2:00 p.m."

Later that day, when the court reconvened, Judge Fletcher ruled that although he was not fully convinced that the state had good standing, he would not forbid them an opportunity to try me again. He then denied our motion for dismissal but granted our motion for a new trial.

"Tony, this is still a win-win for us," Attorney Nuefeld said after the court provided its ruling. "I know you were looking forward to being released today, but I promise you, we will fight this with all we got to the end."

I thanked him and Attorney Morrison before we departed.

The court set the new trial date about sixty days after. Though I had done over twenty-four years in prison on this case, that sixty days felt like forever. I was so ready for it to be over that I fainted. I later awoke in the court bullpen and was treated by a nurse. She provided me with two cups of water, instructed me to stay hydrated, and told the court marshals I was good to go.

CHAPTER 18

Because the judge had reversed my first-degree murder conviction, I was no longer a state prisoner. However, county prison officials said I still had to go through the process, which meant I had to take the four-and-a-half-hour drive back up to SCI Huntingdon to sign out, and then I'd be brought back down after and housed at CFCF.

At this point, I felt like a piece of meat being pulled so many ways by the state. They sure knew how to break you down.

When I arrived at Huntingdon, I was released into the general population and sent back to A-Block.

The next morning, the sergeant informed me that the unit manager needed to see me. Shortly thereafter, the unit manager provided me with a list of steps I needed to take to sign out. I stopped at medical and the library, where they checked to see if I had any overdue books or owed any funds for other costs. Once clear, I made it over to commissary and then the education department.

That afternoon, I made it out to the recreation yard to see my crew. They gave me cigarettes, coffee, and other items I would need to get by.

The next morning, however, two prison guards approached my cell followed by a lieutenant named Hall.

"Mr. Wright, we got to take you to the hole," Lieutenant Hall insisted.

"For what?" I replied. "I'm just here to sign out."

"That exactly. The thing is you're no longer a state prisoner, so we can't have you in the general population. If something happens to you, that's our ass."

"All right ... give me a minute to get situated," I replied, disappointed. I hated the hole. The isolation drove me nuts, as did the lack of ability to freely walk around.

After a few days in the hole, I was transferred back to CFCF. After being in state prisons for nearly twenty-five years, I had to adjust to the county jail. Unlike the six-to-eight hours of state visits, the visits in the county were only thirty minutes. As soon as Darnell and Anthony Jr. came in to visit, it was time for them to leave. I made a grievance complaint to the warden concerning the brief duration of the visits considering I would be preparing for trial and never got a reply.

I further had to get accustomed to living with two other men in a cell after spending nearly two decades in a one-man cell. However, after all the obstacles the detectives, the DA, and the system put me through, I refused to give up. I had to win this trial, and I prayed that my attorneys could paint the vivid picture of me being framed to the jury so they could see the truth.

Two weeks later, Attorney Morrison came to visit me.

"How are you making out in this place, Tony?"

"Honestly, terrible," I replied, watching her closely.

"I understand. I knew it would be a big change for you; that's why I decided to step up and see you."

"You have become more than an attorney to me. You have become a friend."

"That's good, Tony. After what you've been through, the least we can do is to give you moral support."

"So, anything new?"

"Yes. Mrs. Talley's killer, Ronnie Byrd, passed away a few days ago in South Carolina."

"Is that right?" I said, surprised. "I don't know whether to be happy or sad—happy that he's gone off this planet after causing so many people so much harm and pain or sad that he didn't have to go through all he put me through and will never have to stand before the court or Mrs. Talley's family to face and pay for what his DNA shows he did."

"It's a shame, Tony. Thing is, he kept committing violent crimes. He was in the custody of the South Carolina Department of Corrections and was transferred to an outside hospital where he died. The cops on this case are partly to blame, and we intend on proving that."

I just shook my head, taking it all in.

"Our investigator said that he lived only a block from Mrs. Talley and was a known neighborhood crack addict."

"That pretty much explains everything."

"Yeah. We also found out that both St. James and Buddy Richardson, who testified against you in the first trial, have passed since you've been away."

"Wow ... so what can the DA do now that his star witnesses are gone?"

"Probably read their first testimonies to the jury."

"That's allowed?" I asked.

"Yes, most judges will allow it as long as the defense had an opportunity to subject them to cross-examination."

"Did the investigator say how they died?"

"I'm not quite sure ... I think he mentioned that Richardson was killed in Alaska," Attorney Morrison replied.

"I guess what goes around comes around."

"My theory is St. James and Richardson were protecting Ronnie Byrd all along and gave your name up in place of his."

"It's possible. The thing is, those detectives should have known they were not to be trusted or believed," I said, thinking of how they testified against me with a cloud of lies.

"Yes," she agreed. "Trial starts next week."

"Are you guys gonna bring your 'A game'?"

"Of course," she assured me and then shook my hand.

CHAPTER 19

The next week, I prepared myself psychologically for trial. The first trial took a lot out of me, particularly being in the county jail environment, where there was little peace. Now being back in the county jail, I saw that hadn't changed. I had two young bucks running in and out of the cell all day when the block was open and couldn't get peace of mind. Then there were fights constantly breaking out, so the block would be on lockdown, and that prohibited my ability to call my family and attorneys and go to the law library to conduct legal research.

In addition, there were constant "shakedowns," which entailed the prison guards searching our unit and cells and subjecting us to a strip search. I always found those to be intrusive. I would have to remove one article of clothing at a time and hand it to the guard until I was completely naked. Next, I was required to open my mouth for the guard to inspect the inside of my mouth, lift my top lip and then bottle lip, and then show him the inside of my ear and behind my ears. Next, I had to extend my arms forward, wiggle my fingers, and then lift my arms to the ear to reveal my armpits. Next, I had to lift my penis for inspection and then my testicles. Next, I had to turn around and lift each foot. Afterward, I was instructed to spread my butt cheeks for an inspection and then squat and cough. What made matters worse was some of these strip searches were conducted in the presence of my cellmates, although they weren't supposed to be. Any and everything was done for the staff's convenience. Other guards would talk dirty or down to you while they made you strip.

After the shakedowns, the cell would look like it had been hit by a tornado, and it would take a good part of the rest of the day to straighten up and put things back in order.

On the first day of trial, I was awoken about 3:30 a.m. by a prison guard and told I had ten minutes to get ready to get on the bus for court. Afterward, I received a breakfast bag that had hard-boiled eggs, bread, and milk, and a prison guard escorted me to intake. About an hour later, I was handcuffed to other detainees headed to the courthouse.

When I finally stepped into the courtroom, I was greeted by Attorneys Peter Nuefeld, Nina Morrison, and Samuel Silverman. This was my dream team.

Judge (I'll refer to him as Murphy for now) was seated on the bench. The courtroom was filled with my family, my supporters, Mrs. Tally's family, the police, and other spectators.

"Counsel for the state and the defense, are there any motions before I get started and bring in the jury pool?" Judge Murphy asked.

"No, Your Honor," DA Williams rose and replied.

"No, Your Honor," Attorney Nuefeld seconded.

"All right, Bailiff, will you bring the jury pool in?" Judge Murphy said.

Moments after, a line of people of all walks of life began filing into the courtroom and were seated in the first three rows of the courtroom.

The judge welcomed the jury, and the jury-picking process, also known as voir dire, began. This was a very important part of the trial because the selection of these individuals would be deciding my fate. I noticed that my attorneys were focused on seating as many women as possible on my jury. I learned from my first trial that women were more sympathetic toward defendants and were the best defense jurors, as were Blacks and Latinos. I further learned that prosecutors moved for white males over thirty-five years of age to seat on the jury because statistics showed that they were more prosecutor prone. At the end, I felt and hoped that any of the twelve human beings seated would be able to see that the police set me up good for this horrible murder.

When voir dire was completed, the attorneys picked twelve jurors and two alternate jurors.

"All right, the Commonwealth may proceed with its opening statement," Judge Murphy announced.

DA Seth Williams rose from his seat with a yellow pad in his hand and walked to the podium.

"Thank you, Your Honor," he began. "Ladies and gentlemen of the jury, this is a first-degree capital murder charge and a rape charge against the defendant Anthony Wright, who is sitting right over there." DA Williams pointed. "The evidence will show that Mr. Wright forced his way into seventy-seven-year-old Mrs. Talley's home in the Nicetown section of Philadelphia on the evening of October 19, 1991. Afterward, Mr. Wright forced Mrs. Talley at knifepoint to her upstairs bedroom and brutally raped her and then stabbed her multiple times in front and in back of her body. Then, he delivered the crushing blow to her face with the back heel of a shoe."

I glanced over at the jurors, and they all were engaged with DA Williams's every word. I wanted to jump up and tell the jury that he was lying through his teeth, that I had never met Mrs. Talley, nor did I ever lay a hand on her, but I kept my composure.

"The evidence will further show," DA Williams continued, "that Mr. Wright stole Mrs. Talley's property from her home after he killed her, which included two televisions that he later sold to two local drug dealers. But, ladies and gentleman, what Anthony Wright didn't know was three young boys were standing on the corner and witnessed him exit the home of Mrs. Talley around the time of her death and saw him wearing the Chicago Bulls shirt, blue jeans, and black Fila shoes. And to make matters worse, Mr. Wright actually confessed to wearing these clothes during this brutal killing when he was questioned by homicide detectives that you will be hearing from and actually signed a nine-page confession. At the conclusion of the evidence presented to you, I submit that there will be no reasonable doubt at all that Anthony Wright raped and murdered Mrs. Talley in cold blood, and I will ask that you return a guilty verdict for first-degree murder. Thank you," DA Williams ended.

I looked over at the jurors and could see that they were processing the first opening statement.

"Counsel Nuefeld, are you ready to proceed?" Judge Murphy asked.

Attorney Nuefeld rose and walked to the podium. "I am, Your Honor. Thank you. Good morning, ladies and gentlemen of the jury.

Mrs. Talley's death, indeed, was the result of a horrible killing. The Commonwealth, however, has the wrong man being tried before you today and has had the wrong man for the last twenty-five years. The evidence without a doubt will show that Anthony Wright was framed by the Philadelphia Police Department," Attorney Nuefeld said with passion. There were murmurs in the courtroom. "Ladies and gentleman," he continued, "in 2001, the Pennsylvania Legislation enacted new DNA testing under Section 9543.1, and with that enactment came advanced DNA testing that proves 100 percent that Anthony Wright was absolutely not responsible for this crime. Evidence will further show that, yes, Anthony Wright signed a confession. However, the important point that the state left out of their opening statement is that the so-called confession was drafted and the details did not come from Anthony Wright, but rather they came from Detective Devlin. Those words in that confession were the words and thoughts of Detective Devlin that he learned from the investigation of the case," Attorney Nuefeld said, making eye contact with each juror one by one. He had their full attention. "They also failed to tell you that the evidence will show that Anthony Wright was threatened in the presence of a group of detectives to sign the confession, which he did not even read, and was under duress at the time of being held for hours with nothing to eat or drink, nor could he speak with his mother as he requested. Ladies and gentleman, after you hear all the evidence, there will be more than reasonable doubt that Anthony Wright is not guilty. Thank you," Attorney Nuefeld ended.

The jurors watched him carefully as he walked back to the defense table, and then I observed a few looking at me.

"Mr. Williams, is the state ready to proceed?" Judge Murphy asked.

"Yes, Your Honor," DA Williams said after rising from his seat. "First, the state moves to enter the testimony of Assistant Medical Examiner Edwin Lieberman, who conducted the autopsy of Mrs. Talley, into evidence. Because Dr. Lieberman is now deceased, we wish to stipulate a pertinent part of his prior testimony and read it to the jury as they see the notes of testimony on the screen for the projector."

"Attorney Nuefeld, any objection?" Judge Murphy asked.

"No objection, Your Honor," Attorney Nuefeld replied.

"Okay, the state may proceed."

DA Williams placed the notes of testimony of Dr. Lieberman onto the glass of the projector. "Ladies and gentleman of the jury, the following is the sworn testimony given by Dr. Lieberman, who conducted the autopsy on Mrs. Talley. Question: Dr. Lieberman, can you testify to the cause of Mrs. Talley's death? Answer: Yes. Mrs. Talley's death was caused by multiple stab wounds, coupled with blunt force injuries. Question: Can you describe what type of weapon would cause these types of stab wounds that Mrs. Talley suffered? Answer: Because of the dimension of the wounds, and their depth of penetration, it is my opinion that they were likely inflicted by a similar class of knife as the knife recovered from the folds of the victim's housecoat. Question: Can you tell us a time of the victim's death? Answer: I could not conclusively determine the time of the victim's death. I estimate that she died sometime within a time period of thirty-six hours before she was pronounced dead at 4:30 p.m. on Saturday, October 19," DA Williams said, removing the notes of testimony from the slide. "That concludes his testimony requested, Your Honor."

"Okay. The state may call its next witness," Judge Murphy instructed.

"The state calls Detective Burke."

Detective Burke appeared in court from the back wearing a two-piece gray suit. He was a white man with short gray hair. After he was sworn in, the judge asked him to be seated.

"Mr. Burke, where you employed with the Philadelphia Police Department?" DA Williams asked.

"Yes."

"How long were you employed there, and what position did you hold last?"

"Thirty-five years, and I became a sergeant of the Philadelphia Homicide Unit before I retired three years ago," Detective Burke answered.

"Do you recall the homicide investigation of Mrs. Louise Talley?"

"Yes, I remember it quite well. Well, because of the age of the victim and the brutal way in which she was killed, it was one of the worst cases I ever was involved in."

"And can you tell the jury what was your involvement in that investigation?"

"I was supervisor of the detectives I assigned to investigate her death."

"And who were those detectives?"

"Detectives Dennis Dusak and Mavel Santiago, and later other detectives helped conduct witness interviews, the interrogation of the defendant, and collecting evidence."

"Okay. Did you go to the crime scene, and if so, can you explain to the jury what you saw when you arrived?"

"Yes, I did go to the crime scene. Detectives Dusak and Santiago and I found the victim upstairs in her bedroom. I recall that she was facedown, underneath a girdle and a house coat. Very bloody scene. I could see a number of stab wounds all over her back, shoulders, and arms. It was really messy. The room also appeared ransacked," Detective Burke described.

"Were any weapons discovered on the scene?"

"Yes. We found a knife that appeared to come from her kitchen that was nearby the body, wrapped up in a pink towel."

"Did you discover any defensive wounds on Mrs. Talley?"

"Yes. We found defense stab wounds on her hands."

"Did there come a time that you learned things were missing from the home?"

"Yes," Mr. Burke responded. "A police officer reported that he received information that two men from the neighborhood—Roland St. James and John 'Buddy' Richardson—were observed trying to sell the victim's televisions, and they were persons of interest."

"Were they located and interviewed?"

"Yes."

"What, if anything, did you learn from their interviews?"

"Both men stated that Anthony Wright was responsible for the rape and stabbing death of the victim."

"Do you see him in the courtroom today?"

"Yes. He is sitting over there."

"Your Honor, please let the record reflect that the witness has identified Mr. Anthony Wright?" DA Williams asked.

"It will so reflect," Judge Murphy assured him.

"Did both said witnesses provide signed statements to your office indicating that Anthony Wright was the killer?"

"Yes."

"Nothing further, Your Honor."

"Mr. Nuefeld?" Judge Murphy said.

"Detective, you said that witnesses St. James and Richardson were the ones in fact in possession of Mrs. Talley's stolen televisions and were first suspects in Mrs. Talley's death, correct?" Attorney Nuefeld asked.

"That's correct."

"Then once they were placed into police custody, they gave Mr. Wright's name as the one responsible for the murder, correct?"

"That's correct."

"So, can you explain to the jury how they went from the first suspects to witnesses?"

"Well ... they were in possession of the stolen televisions and admitted to selling them. But they also said it was Mr. Wright who committed the rape and murder."

"So, receiving and selling stolen property is a crime. Is it not?"

"Yes, it is," Detective Burke replied.

"So, why weren't they charged with those crimes?"

"Well … a decision was made not to prosecute those crimes because they became witnesses."

"And who made that decision?"

"Objection, Your Honor. The detective should not be required to disclose that information," DA Williams stood up and said.

"Your Honor, there's nothing privileged about who made the decision," Attorney Nuefeld countered.

"I agree. Answer the question, Detective," Judge Murphy responded.

"Well, the decision was made by myself and the district attorney's office."

"Who in the district attorney's office, Detective?" Attorney Nuefeld asked, agitated.

"District Attorney … Williams," Detective Burke conceded.

There were murmurs in the courtroom.

"Detective, isn't it true that St. James and Richardson could have just given you Mr. Wright's name just so they wouldn't go to jail for their admitted crimes?" Attorney Nuefeld asked, staring the detective down.

"I don't think that was the case."

"Why is that?"

"They appeared to be telling the truth."

"Well, was there any other evidence corroborating that they even knew Anthony Wright?"

"No … there was not."

"And you knew that both Mr. St. James and Mr. Richardson had rather extensive criminal convictions."

"Yes, I did."

"And you just took their words for it?"

"Yes. A lot of credible information we received came from convicted felons."

"However, Detective, in this case, did your office ever receive credible information from St. James and Richardson that led to an arrest of any other suspect of a crime?"

"No, not to my knowledge," Detective Burke conceded.

I watched the jury observe this exchange intently.

"Now, Detective," Attorney Nuefeld continued, "but is it also true that you released both St. James and Richardson from custody at that time?"

"Yes, it is."

"Isn't it true that John Richardson had an outstanding warrant at the time your office brought him into your custody?"

"Yes, in a different matter."

"Can you explain to this jury why you let a man out of jail when you knew he had an outstanding warrant?" Attorney Nuefeld questioned fiercely.

"Uh ... well, it wasn't a decision made by myself."

"Did District Attorney Williams authorize this decision?"

"Uh ... I don't really recall."

"Well, you didn't have the authority to release someone from custody that has an outstanding warrant, right?"

"Not unless I received authorization from the DA's office."

"And did you obtain any authorization to do so?"

"Not that I can recall."

"But you did it anyway."

"Yes."

"Nothing further, Your Honor," Attorney Nuefeld ended.

"Any redirect?" Judge Murphy asked.

"Just briefly, Your Honor," Assistant DA Reynolds got up and replied.

"Detective, when witnesses St. James and Richardson both informed you that Mr. Wright was responsible for Mrs. Talley's death, did they give you any reason to doubt their information?" ADA Reynolds asked.

"No, they did not."

"Thank you. Nothing further, Your Honor."

"Any recross?"

"No, Your Honor."

"Okay. This seems like a good time to take a recess. We will break for lunch. This court is adjourned until 1:00 p.m. this afternoon," Judge Murphy instructed and then banged his gavel.

I looked back at my family, and they nodded, indicating they approved of my defense team's performance. I knew there was more work to do, and I had to prepare myself mentally to take the stand if need be. This would be a fight to the end.

CHAPTER 20

When court reconvened at 1:00 p.m. DA Williams came out swinging. He called Detective Dusak to the stand to tell the jury about my signing the confession.

"Detective, during the interrogation of the defendant, would you say he was threatened in any way?"

"No, not at all."

"Did he confess to the stabbing and killing of Mrs. Talley voluntarily?"

"Yes," Detective Dusak answered.

"And did he include details that only the killer would have known?"

"Yes."

"Can you give us an example, Detective?"

"Well, he said he was wearing a black Chicago Bulls shirt, blue jeans, and black Fila shoes during the crime and hid these items at his house, underneath his bed!"

These detectives were so good at lying, they should have been actors because they were delivering an Oscar performance that I hoped we would rip apart.

"Did you subsequently obtain a search warrant and conduct a search of his home?" DA Williams asked.

"No. Detective Jastrzembski did."

"All right. Was the defendant under duress when he signed the nine-page confession?"

"No. Absolutely not."

"Your Honor, may I approach?"

"You may."

DA Williams approached the witness stand with the confession.

"Detective, I would like you to take a look at this document, and please inform me if you recognize it."

Detective Dusak looked over the document. "I do."

"What is this document?" DA Williams asked.

"This is the nine-page confession that Anthony Wright signed."

"Your Honor, the state moves to have this document admitted into evidence for the jury's review."

"It shall be admitted," Judge Murphy responded.

"Detective, did Anthony Wright sign this confession to killing Mrs. Louise Talley on October 19 of his own free will?"

"Yes, he did."

"Nothing further, Your Honor."

"The defense," Judge Murphy said.

"Thank you, Your Honor," Attorney Morrison said as she rose from her seat.

"Detective, how long would you say the interrogation of Anthony Wright took place?"

"A few hours."

"Well, that's a pretty long time, is it not?"

"It's average."

"Well, how many times did you ask him if he committed this crime?"

"I'm not certain; I would imagine a lot."

"Is it fair to say that within the first hour of the interrogation, he denied committing this crime?"

"Yes."

"Well, how many times does a person have to deny committing a crime before they are allowed to leave by you?"

"Until ... I'm satisfied that they're telling the truth."

"So, according to you, if someone told you three hundred times that they didn't commit a crime in the course of several hours, and you felt they were lying, you still wouldn't release them if you had nothing to establish probable cause to charge them?"

"I wouldn't have any choice."

"Detective, can you tell us how many detectives were present during this interrogation?"

"It was Detective Devlin, Sergeant Burke, and myself."

"And isn't it true that Detective Devlin got into Mr. Wright's face and threatened to 'skull-fuck' Mr. Wright if he didn't sign the confession?"

"I don't recall that."

"And isn't it true that you placed your hands on the back of his neck during Detective Devlin threatening Mr. Wright?"

"No."

"Would you admit it to this jury if it were true?"

"Uh … I wouldn't have a choice, Counsel. I swore to tell the truth."

"Even if the truth meant that you and your fellow detective committed a number of violations that could cost both of you your careers?"

"Yes."

EPILOGUE

After my acquittal, I had to adjust to being back in society. So much had changed in twenty-five years that I knew that I had to take it slow and easy.

I spent a lot of time with the family and getting to know my grandchildren.

The Innocence Project holds a lot of events, enlightening society and communities of the horrors of the criminal justice system. I've been invited to speak at several events all over the nation.

Many times, when I share my story, there's not a dry eye in the room. I tell kids all the time, "Don't give a statement to the police under any circumstances unless you have your attorney and parents present, and they agree it's in your best interest. Because if you do otherwise, they'll surely use it against you."

I tell parents, "Teach and train your kids. If you let the streets teach them, then what?" The street can be very dangerous. Jail is not cool. Jail is not gangsta. Don't be stupid and go to jail. Don't be stupid and get shot by the police. Life is too short. Don't waste your life. See me, I spent twenty-five years in prison for a crime I did not commit. I lost my mom, good friends, and the joy of watching my son grow into a man while I was in there. You must understand the American system so you know how to avoid getting caught up in it. I'm not saying that all cops are bad, but I'm not saying that all are good. You'll have to decide that by their actions. When they say, "Let me see those hands,' they mean it, or they'll kill you dead. It's been dark, and it's still happening all around us. Life is precious. Live it, love it, and enjoy it. Don't count yourselves out. They counted me out. But count yourselves in, and keep hope alive!